Pornography is a Murderer

The Suicide of the Soul

David D. Edgington, PhD.

Learn more at

www.CompassionateCounselors.com

Matthew 22:37 Books

Phoenix, Arizona 85013

Recommendations

"No amount of law or legalism will free someone from the grips of lust." Dr. David Edgington's book is timely, full of wisdom and offers help for the heart that feels dominated and crushed by the grips of pornography and warnings for the heart that is blinded to the dangers of it. The depiction of Pornography being both murderous and suicidal toward the soul is a confronting wake up call to the reality of this deadly snare. Courageously, Dr. Edgington warns of the dangers, pitfalls and consequences of pornography's bondage. He reminds us who the real enemy is and that our fight is not against flesh and blood but against a notorious and dangerous adversary, the devil. Dr. Edgington gives insight and tools to gain joy and find victory in the battle. He declares that HOPE and FREEDOM are through the "Abounding Grace" of God available in Christ Jesus by walking in the power of the Holy Spirit. Reading this book may just save your life!

Pastor Kevin King,

Bethel Bible Church, Queen Creek, AZ

To God be the Glory! This book is a much-needed tool to help one battle the powers of evil at work in today's modern society. This is an outreach to those who are struggling with the temptation of modern pornography. As a 24 year-old Pastor's son, I know how devastating and intimidating this particular evil can be. Too many young men who become hopeless and trapped in despair can feel comforted to know that Dr. Edgington has written this book to encourage, reaffirm, and remind us of our stand for God, and His stand with us. The Bible is Power! And this book asserts the Bible and shows that even the modern-day schemes of the devil can NEVER prevail against the Hope that is in us, or against the everlasting Word of God. An enriching read for all believers, young and old!

(Anonymous)

Recommendations

After forty years of preaching and counseling, I can affirm that sexual immorality in the form or pornography is indeed a murderer, bringing suicide to the soul. Some years ago, I received a phone call from a Christian who literally had a rope around his neck and was preparing to jump off a chair to end his life. He was trapped in pornography and could see no hope.

David does a masterful job of pointing us to the biblical solutions to overcome this sin. God's solution is best summed in Dr. Edgington's statement. *"The key to success in our fight against pornography is for God to change our hearts through the Word of God."*

Whether you are a Pastor, Counselor or a Christian fighting pornography, picking up this book is your first step in understanding and helping you find victory and long-lasting freedom.

Jerry Selvidge,
Pastor and Counselor
Jesus First! Church, Phoenix, AZ

Recommendations

Pornography is a Murderer is such an apt title. The cold hand of sinful death has been felt in many a home and relationship including mine. I have felt its blade kill godly joy, faith in the promises of God, steadfast trust in the finished work of Christ. Would you take fire into your bosom and not be burned? Oh how the conscience is seared! Guilt, hopelessness, futility, joylessness, lovelessness are all frequent companions.

But He is faithful! His Word thrusts through like a ray of light in the deepest dark. Oh run servant of the most High God! Go to His Word and soak! Though the seared callous scars may seem impenetrable, the Spirit of God can, will, and desires greatly to heal and restore!

I have been fighting this sin for 30 plus years and it seems like I have had more failures than victories but God, through faithful men fighting alongside me and encouraging me, will see this through to glory!

I praise God for this resource by Dr. Edgington and the clear concise wartime strategies in battling this enemy. I praise God for you, Pastor!

Benjamin Partin,
Queen Creek, AZ

Recommendations

Dr. David Edgington says, *"The title of this book may seem contradictory - porn 'murders' yet your soul commits 'suicide'. So, which is it- murder or suicide? Actually it is both. There is no contradiction here - the enemy of our souls uses pornography to "murder" us, yet it is we ourselves who hang ourselves with it."*

But as deadly as pornography is there is hope of escape from this sin through the grace of our Lord Jesus Christ. Dr. Edgington, a NANC certified biblical counselor since 1995, writes from both his years of experience and his intimate knowledge of using the Holy Scriptures, the sword of the Spirit, to set the captive free. This small book, is more than another "how to" manual to put in with your other counseling books. It is a gift from God to be treasured by those so easily entangled with this sin. Having read this book one will certainly walk away thankful for God's word of grace which is able to build you up and to give you the inheritance among all those who are sanctified. (Acts 20:32).

Pastor Bill Phillips,
King of Kings Church, Goodyear, AZ

Table of Contents

Preface

I'm generally not a fan of statistics since survey questions can be framed in such a manner so that you get the result that you want (Mark Twain popularized a famous saying about their dubious nature – "Lies, D--- lies and statistics"). They can be easily twisted to mean what you want them to mean to "prove" your point. But if the numbers below are even *half* right, it would still shock us. And these numbers bear up to what I see in doing biblical counseling with hurting souls every day. So I reluctantly and sadly believe what these statistics tell us. They are stunning, and they should absolutely stagger us. Don't skip over them, they tell you just how serious this problem is that this book addresses. Here are just a few of the many statistics[1] that are available.

•In 2016, people watched 4.6 *billion hours* of pornography *at just one pornographic website.* If you put that in terms of years instead of hours, it works out to 524,000 years.

•In 2013, pornography sites received more traffic than Amazon, Netflix and Twitter *combined.*[2]

•96% of young adults are encouraging, accepting, or neutral in their views regarding pornography.

•32% of young adults say "viewing pornography" is "usually or always wrong," compared to 56% who say that "recycling" is "usually or always wrong."[3]

---

[1] Most of these statistics are from an in depth study done by The Barna Group, *The Porn Phenomenon* – the *Impact of Pornography in the Digital Age,* (Ventura, CA: Barna, 2016) and done in partnership with Josh Mc-Dowell ministries.

[2] www.charismanews.com/sponsored-content/67015-what-the-porn-indus-try-doesn-t-want-you-to-find-out accessed on 8/28/17.

[3] www.focusonthefamily.com/socialissues/citizen-magazine/the-porn-phe-nomenon accessed 5/1/2017.

•70% of pornography is watched on a mobile phone in the US.

•80% of pornography viewers feel no guilt about what they are doing.

•1 in 5 Youth Pastors and 1 in 7 Senior Pastors use pornography.[4]

These figures should stun us. They should also arrest our attention so that we weep over this ubiquitous threat that is rarely discussed. A thinking man would ask, *"Why isn't pornography illegal"*? There are many excuses regarding why it is still legal, but no good reasons why it is not. If you are over age 35 (in 2017), you probably don't realize how deadly pornography is for the youth of our society since you did not grow up with the Internet in the Digital Age. Those under age 35 (in the year of this publication in 2017) have had exposure to pornography in a way that middle-aged people cannot truly grasp.

As has been said, the pornography crisis is not coming, it is already here. It used to come in the mail wrapped in discreet packaging, now it is on the computer you carry in your pocket (your smart phone).[5]

---

[4] www.georgepwood.com/2016/05/03/review-of-the-porn-phenomenon-by-barna-group/ accessed on 5/1/2017.

[5] www.barna-resources.myshopify.com/products/porn-phenomenon accessed on 5/1/2017

Introduction

Pornography is a cold-blooded killer. It does not care if you are a newlywed, or been married for decades. Pornography murders romance since it permits no rivals. It kills a marriage since it lures one spouse into the digital bed of another. Pornography leaves no room for competition. The enemy of our souls is said to be a murderer (John 8:44) so it should not surprise us that one of his weapons of destruction is pornography. Pornography does not perform its execution in one fell swoop, but patiently works on devouring the soul little by little – just like the devil does (1 Peter 5:8). Sin is also described as a "killer" in Romans 7:10-11 as it "seizes an opportunity" in the unsuspecting soul. Eventually the sin associated with pornography assassinates any semblance of romance in a marriage. The relationship won't be serious for very long. I cringe when I hear people say their struggle is "only" with pornography – not actual sex with a living person. I have counseled men who have gone on pornography binges of 10 to 12 consecutive hours. And then they do the same thing the next day. And the next. I've never counseled a man who has been committing the physical act of adultery for 10 to 12 non-stop hours – nor have I ever heard of one. We minimize pornography to our own peril.

But pornography also entails the suicide of the soul. It's as if the devil has put the noose before our souls and beckons us to indulge in some "fun." As the noose hangs before our souls, we are deceived into thinking that slipping our neck into it will be good for us. We willingly put our head through the loop in the rope and let it slide gently around our necks. We tighten the knot around our throats. And then we jump off the platform. We do it all of our own free will. No one puts the noose around our neck. No one tightens the knot. And no one pushes us off of the platform. Viewing pornography is not the devil's fault – though he is masterful at knowing how to tempt you with it. We view pornography because we *want* to view it. If we would picture the viewing of pornography as the hanging of our souls, we would *never* do it. But instead, we allow ourselves to be deceived and jump off with both feet.

If you view yourself as a "victim" of pornography, you will not find freedom. If you believe you are helpless in the face of this foe, you will not find hope. If you think God hasn't helped you enough, you don't know God as well as you think you do. If you see this as an "unwanted" temptation, then you don't understand your own heart. Unless your heart changes, none of your behavior will change for very long. I see it every day in counseling hurting and lost souls. The ones who merely institute rules, put filters on their phones, have an "accountability" partner and make outward behavioral changes never see their change last for very long. But the ones whose hearts truly change by the power of God using the Word of God – the ones who truly deal with their own lusts, their own demands, their own temper tantrums, their own entitlement mindset – these are the ones who find freedom and peace and contentment and joy in the Holy Spirit. The good news has to be grasped as "the best news ever" not merely as facts to which we assent. The Holy Spirit has to be welcomed and powerfully residing in and filling your soul. God's amazing grace must be seen in its "abounding abundance" (far, far more than you "need") not simply as information or as intellectual facts. The idols have to be smashed and obliterated. The reality of spiritual warfare needs to not only be respected, but also strategically fought by the weapons of God not the weapons of our flesh (2 Corinthians 10:3-4).

You *can* overcome the lure of pornography. Don't let it murder you. You don't *have to* view it. Don't kill your own soul. My deepest desire is that this book will lead you to find the freedom that can only come through seeking the Lord Jesus Christ through the Word of God by means of the Spirit of God

Soli Deo Gloria

Chapter 1

Conviction or Condemnation?

I have counseled many men who have struggled with pornography to such a degree that they believe that God will never forgive them for what they have done. Their souls have consumed so much pornography that they doubt their own salvation. They say, "If I keep getting dragged into porn, how could I possibly be saved? A true believer knows better than to do this."

This is not an easy issue to address and I don't want to give simplistic "saved or unsaved" answers here. For many men, the guilt on their souls is incredibly deep and painful and persistent. For such men that wrestle with guilt, I'd suggest you view this through the following lens:

Remember that the Holy Spirit brings "conviction" but the devil brings "condemnation."

When we sin, we should "feel" something. There may be sorrow, shame, regret, or guilt. But surely something is happening in our souls when we fail. We know there is forgiveness through the cross of Jesus Christ. But we don't want to make light of our sin either. We know there is hope in the good news, but we don't want to think little of our disobedience. This balancing act is where the devil often lurks. He knows some Christians have a tender conscience, so he works his guilt and his condemnation on them. He knows other Christians think little of their sin, so he affirms them in their indifference to holiness.

14

The key here is to maintain gospel centered hope without minimizing sin. It is at times a difficult balance to maintain because often the "feeling" is the same in "conviction" as it is in "condemnation."

The Holy Spirit works in the soul in such a way that sin is never minimized. There must be some[6] degree of sorrow and regret in regards to our sin. We should never be cavalier about it. Yet at the same time, there should be "hope" in the soul. The Holy Spirit brings hope for change. He brings hope for forgiveness. He brings hope for conquering sin. That's not being naïve, that's believing in the power of the Holy Spirit. Most men caught in the grips of pornography have little to no hope of ever being free from its clutches. Brothers, *hear* what the Word of God says.

The Scriptures remind us:

"If we confess our sins, He is faithful and just to forgive us our sins and to cleanse us from all unrighteousness." (1 John 1:9)

"I acknowledged my sin to You, and I did not cover my iniquity; I said, I will confess my transgressions to the LORD, and You forgave the iniquity of my sin." (Psalm 32:5)

"But thanks be to God, that you who were (past tense) once slaves of sin have become (now!) obedient from the heart to the standard of teaching to which you were committed and having been set free from sin, have become (now!) slaves of righteousness." (Romans 6:17-18)

"And when He (the Holy Spirit) comes, He will convict the world concerning sin and righteousness and judgment." (John 16:8)

---

[6] I use the word "some" here because it is tempting to try to quantify just how much sorrow one must feel in the soul. No one can discern "just how much" sorrow there should be, nor can anyone say this is "enough" sorrow, or for that matter "not enough" sorrow. Each man will be different and it is best to leave this to the Holy Spirit's unique operations on each soul.

The devil, on the other hand, does pretty much the opposite of what we see in those passages. If you tend to be more indifferent to your sin, then he will help you to continue to make light of your sin – he wants you to think that your sin is not really a big problem, so repentance is not really necessary. Jesus died and paid for all your sins, plus He forgives you. So why be concerned about your sin? But if you are indifferent to your sin involving pornography, it is unlikely that you will be picking up this book to read it. So that tactic of the enemy probably doesn't apply to you.

On the other hand, if you are someone who dwells on your sin too much, then the devil will take a different approach with you. He wants you to feel condemnation for your sin. He wants you to think there is no hope for you and there is no possibility of change. He wants to keep you a slave to sin. He wants you to think that you might as well keep indulging yourself because you're just going to go back to this sin anyway. And he'll either convince you to "keep sinning because you are forgiven" or "don't bother crying out for help from Jesus since you are not really a believer anyway." It's a masterful plan. He is clever, shrewd and unfortunately very often he is effective.

His attempts at condemnation are calculating and strategic. They are not haphazard. He is not "random" or "aimless." He has strategies and schemes by which he can trip up the unsuspecting believer.

"...so that we would not be outwitted by Satan; for we are not ignorant of his designs." (2 Corinthians 2:11)

"Put on the whole armor of God, that you may be able to stand against the schemes of the devil. For we do not wrestle against flesh and blood..." (Ephesians 6:11-12a)

"...fall into the condemnation of the devil..." (1 Timothy 3:6)

He tried strategies and schemes with both Peter and Job. His temptations worked with Peter in leading him away from remaining faithful during a time of intense testing, and in Job the enemy's hatred can practically be felt as the devil attempted to destroy a man who is "blameless, upright and fears God and turns away from evil." (Job 1:1).

"Simon, Simon, behold, Satan demanded to have you (plural – all of the disciples), *that he might sift you* (plural – all of the disciples) *like wheat, but I have prayed for you* (singular – Peter) *that your* (singular – Peter) *faith may not fail. And when you* (singular – Peter) *have turned again, strengthen your* (singular – Peter) *brothers."* (Luke 22:31-32)

"Then Satan answered the Lord and said, 'Skin for skin! All that a man has he will give for his life. But stretch out Your hand and touch his bone and his flesh, and he will curse You to Your face." (Job 2:4-5)

Yet both of these fallible men found restoration through the beautiful mercy of God. As we know, Jesus publicly restored Peter with His thrice-repeated reminder of "love" for Jesus (John 21:15-19). And Job was vindicated when God identified Job as being the one "speaking what is right" about God unlike his friends had done (Job 42:7-8). God would not restore Job's friends until he prayed for them (Job 42:8-9).

Though the devil did not have the last word in either of these men's lives, his condemnation of them both is nearly palpable. We will cover more in regards to spiritual warfare in Chapter 6.

I cannot prove this, but I would suspect that pornography is one of the easiest sins for men in our day to fall into – especially young men.

A few years ago I spoke at a men's retreat where there was a large group of teenage high school boys. These young men were honest with me since they trusted that I would not divulge their "secrets." Every one of them said that they had viewed pornography. And these were not "unchurched" kids, or kids that came from bad homes or had absentee parents. I knew their Moms and Dads and knew these young men were from godly homes. Several were PK's (Pastor's Kids). Yet every single young man admitted to me that he had viewed pornography. A few of my own sons were in that group – and I knew by first hand knowledge what they had been taught about the deadly trap of pornography and the beauty of sexual purity. Yet even they had given in to the ubiquitous temptation that existed in their young lives.

I grew up in the 60's and 70's when pornography had to be discovered in a magazine because there was no Internet. You had to work at it to "find" pornography or you'd have to be willing to humiliate yourself and buy it in a store. Now we have pocket computers (smart phones) that not only make pornography readily available, but also can give it to us absolutely free. And now there is *video* acting out sexual sin, not "just" photos. The temptation is frequently too much for a young man to resist.[7] It makes me grateful that I didn't grow up with this sin so easily within reach. Technological advance is wonderful and should be encouraged, but it also makes it easier (more "convenient") for the heart of man to sin. I would suspect that within a few years of the publication of this book, much of the technological things I have covered will be out of date. It is not too difficult to foresee how "virtual sex" or interactive "sex androids" will be the next wave of sexual sin problems we face.

---

[7] Young women are increasingly using pornography. See below.

In a recent survey, 1/3 of men did not think that having sex with a robot/android was "cheating."[8] Though sex androids are not yet widespread as I write this in 2017, the day in the not-too-distant-future is coming when they will be as common as a housecat. That day is not here yet – but it is close.

---

[8] www.foxnews.com/tech/2017/10/04/get-set-for-sex-robot-revolution-survey-says.html accessed on 10/5/17.

Chapter 2

Killing the Beauty of Sex

Pornography is not a friend. It will only lead to heartache, pain and broken relationships in a marriage. Here are some further potted[9] thoughts about why it is so troubling to our souls.

1) Pornography is not <u>reality</u>.

It is fictional and not true-to-life. It is an image on a screen or a magazine. It is a video of someone else whom you have never met nor will you ever meet. No one cares what the woman's name is, nor does anyone care about anything about her life. It is not a real person that is in your presence but a representation of that person where no true relationship can possibly exist. As such, it is a type of "idolatry of the imagination." It is a fantasy, but also a fantasy that is detached from reality.

2) Pornography builds false <u>expectations</u>.

The fantasy life that some develop as a result of viewing pornography becomes so strong and powerful that nothing can ever match this or live up to the expectation. A real life spouse will be intimidated by such lofty and unrealistic expectations.

---

[9] "Potted" in the sense of "put into a short and easily assimilable form."

A wife will feel demoralized if she is compared to shapely models who have personal trainers or starve themselves to remain thin, and a man will be emasculated who is compared to a steroid-enhanced beefcake, or professional body-builder.

3) Pornography is a <u>selfish</u> means to gain sexual satisfaction.

Pornography is the source that men turn to in order to gain their own satisfaction but who fail to see God's design being primarily for you to give your *spouse* sexual satisfaction. It is a selfish display of self-gratification rather than loving service to your spouse. We are urged to "deny ourselves daily" (Luke 9:23), yet this is what the man gripped by pornography is unwilling to do. Also, we should not assume that this is just a male problem. In fact, it is estimated that 30% of Internet pornography is now viewed by women.[10] This is no longer only a male sin but now the push for equality has brought it out into the open for women to have lusts and commit sins just like men. In addition to this, men and women *both* can struggle with pornography in a different way. Men will tend to "view" pornography, but women can tend to "commit" pornography.[11]

When women dress in a provocative manner to arouse the sexual desire of men, they are committing pornography with their own bodies. Men may lust after women in obvious ways, but women fall into lust when they dress (or undress) because they know what catches a man's eye.

When women dress in a manner to show more skin and cleavage, this is not merely a "fashion statement."

---

[10] John Piper, "Sex and the Supremacy of Christ: Part Two," in *Sex and the Supremacy of Christ*, ed. John Piper and Justin Taylor (Wheaton: Crossway, 2005), 44.

[11] Joshua Harris, *Sex is Not the Problem (Lust is)* (Colorado Springs: Multnomah, 2003), 87.

When Scripture (1 Timothy 2:9) urges women to dress in "respectable apparel" and "with modesty and self-control" it is describing a massive temptation – women can easily clothe their bodies to captivate the attention of men.

4) Pornography is the lazy way to gain sexual satisfaction.

No relationship is developed with a pornographic image. This is why pornography is so easy, but also it is why it tempts the slothful man. The photos and videos will never say no. They will never be too tired. They will never be sick. Never be too busy. Never be pre-occupied. Never had a long day with the kids. Never have "time-of-the-month" problems. They will never lack interest in sex. They will always be available. This is why pornography is an example of "cheating" at sex. It is the lazy way to sexual satisfaction.

Proverbs 20:4 says, *"The sluggard does not plow in the autumn; he will seek at harvest and have nothing."*

The sluggard does not want to expend the effort to plow his fields so that he will reap a harvest later. Likewise, the sluggard does not want to expend the effort that is necessary for a relationship with a real live woman. The sluggard always has an excuse for why he is viewing pornography. His wife is "cold," he has sexual "needs" that aren't being met, he "couldn't help himself," or "it is impossible to avoid porn in today's world."

But the sluggard will reap the fruit of his sin.[12] His relationship with his wife will be dramatically affected and there will not only be a coldness from his wife, but his own desires for her will turn cold.

---

[12] Charles Bridges, *An Exposition of the Book of Proverbs* (New York: Robert Carter and Brothers, 1865; reprint, Lexington, KY: Forgotten Books), 283 (page citations are to the reprint edition).

5) Pornography <u>dishonors</u> the marriage relationship and defrauds your spouse

According to Hebrews 13:4 *"Let marriage be held in honor among all, and let the marriage bed ("koite") be undefiled, for God will judge the sexually immoral and adulterous."* Though our culture does not honor marriage any longer, it should be concerning to us that the Church does not honor it as highly any longer either. Divorce is rampant in the church today. How many people born since 1985 will have 50-year marriages? Very few, I'm afraid. Pre-marital sex is so commonplace that we rarely are shocked to hear about it anymore. Gender confusion is so common that previous black-and-white-issues are now being discussed and debated rather than being crystal clear. Just the fact that there is even a "discussion" about which bathroom men and women should use tells us that we have fallen in an unprecedented way. It should not surprise us then, to find that pornography has such a tight grip on God's people. The Church has lost much of its influence upon the world because the world has had such a profound influence upon the Church. We can rightly ask, "Is the Church in the world, or is the world in the Church?" The word in (4) for "bed" is the Greek word "koite" (koe-ee'-tay) which is similar to our English word "coitus" (koe-ee'-tus) which means sexual intercourse. So we could say, "Let marital sex be honorable and undefiled." It is not to become sinful, not soiled by another man or woman, not degraded by pornography, by voyeurism, or selfish motives.

Neither the husband nor the wife should be asked to perform a sex act that the other finds distasteful or uncomfortable. There is nothing in Scripture, for instance, that forbids oral sex, yet if one or the other is reluctant in this area, there should be no pressure to do so. Caring and gentleness and the desire not to offend should guide the thinking here. Pornography does not allow the marriage to be guided by these principles.

Also notice the word of judgment that is included here. There are consequences to sexual immorality that must not be taken lightly. Those consequences may be in this life or in the life to come. God is described as the "avenger" (1 Thessalonians 4:6-7) and the Giver of wrath due to sexual immorality (Ephesians 5:5-6) and his sin will not go "unpunished" (Proverbs 6:29). You also want to wrestle with Hebrews 12:15-17 and see that this is indeed a point where you will find "no chance to repent, though (you seek for) it with tears." Where is "that point"? How much sin? How many times do I fall and then find that God will not come back? We must realize that there is a point where it is "too late," when you are no longer able to repent - yet none of us knows when that is.[13] God deliberately keeps such questions unanswered so as to build in our hearts a biblical fear of Him. But those indulged in sexual sin have little fear of God. Far too many act in a manner as if this sin does not bring any lasting harm. We believe this to our own peril.

6) Pornography harms marital intimacy.

All that we are speaking about in this book is attempting to move toward fostering marital intimacy.[14] Pornography, however, does nothing to encourage intimacy but rather undermines and destroys it. Many husbands wonder at the lack of sexual interest that their wives display. It is common for men to not see the connection between *relational* intimacy and *sexual* intimacy. If you do not have the first, you will not have the second. And pornography slowly undermines the joy and satisfaction that can come through sexual intercourse.

---

[13] See www.desiringgod.org/interviews/has-my-sexual-sin-made-me-unsavable accessed on 3/24/17.

[14] For a fuller treatment of intimacy in marriage, please see my upcoming book, "Romance is Not Foreplay" available soon on www.Amazon.com

Men often silently wonder (or not so silently…) "why isn't my wife more interested in sex?" and wives may think about "why does my husband talk about our budget but never about what is pleasing in lovemaking?" These thoughts may lodge in the mind, yet never get expressed – especially if relational intimacy is not carefully cultivated.[15]

7) Pornography <u>Sabotages</u> the Thought Life

What the mind dwells on will shape and affect the heart. This is why "biblical meditation" is so powerful and it can be a blessed means of grace.[16]

This is also why it can be a devastating soul killer. In the span of just a few verses in Ephesians 4, the unregenerate mind is described in ways that should give us all pause since many believers wrestle with the lure of pornography in these very same areas. It speaks of the "futility of our minds" (4:17). In other words, there is a definitive hopelessness and futility about our minds. Every effort put forth to attain happiness will end in disappointment[17] - just like what happens with pornography. They are "darkened in their understanding" (4:18). This means that the light of God is absent in this mind. Physical blindness is bad, but spiritual blindness is far worse since spiritually blind people are blind to their own blindness.[18]

---

[15] Gary and Betsy Ricucci, *Love that Lasts* (Wheaton: Crossway, 2006), 133-134.

[16] For a fuller treatment of this see my book, "The Beauty of Biblical Meditation," available on www.Amazon.com

[17] William Hendriksen, *New Testament Commentary: Exposition of Ephesians* (Grand Rapids: Baker, 1967), 209.

[18] Paul David Tripp, *Instrument in the Redeemer's Hand* (Phillipsburg, NJ: P & R Publishing, 2002), 279.

Our minds are also "given up to sensuality, greedy to practice every kind of impurity" (4:19), which reminds us that we all demand more than we should. My "rights" and "feelings" become paramount and easily lead me into more depravity.[19]

Letting thoughts linger is one of the dangers in the thought life. We deceptively think we are "strong enough" to handle these passing thoughts. But this is precisely why the Scriptures urge us to *"put to death...sexual immorality"* (Colossians 3:5) and to *"put off your old self, which belongs to your former manner of life and is corrupt through deceitful desires"* (Ephesians 4:22). Did you catch that? The desires are "real," but they are "deceitful" – they fool us into thinking that they will satisfy us. We need to not only stop feeding the sin, we need to strike a death blow to it, before it kills us. It is a war. We must not allow our souls to be murdered by this ruthless killer.

One of the problems we have with our thoughts is that we don't always want the lustful thoughts to go away.[20] We may "say" we want it gone, but do we? We may be like Augustine when he was trying to overcome sexual sin. He said to the Lord,

---

[19] As I write this, women are marching and wearing female sex organs as "hats," (and giving the hats vulgar names) and wearing full body suits in the shape of female genitalia with faux pubic hair. Does this advance the respect that women desire? Does this "empower" women, or bring them to open shame? What if men paraded in the streets dressed as a male sex organ – how would we react to this? This female/male double standard does not advance the discussion to anywhere helpful. It simply puts on open display the darkened mind that we see in Ephesians 4:17-19. The mind of women is just as darkened as that of men since the image of God is fallen in both. We have to stop thinking of women as the "fairer sex." That may have been generally true in a different cultural climate, but it is no longer accurate to think in those terms. In fact, to think otherwise is the epitome of sexism.

[20] Pure Life Ministries Email "How to Fight for a Lust Free Mind," by Ed Buch, September 21, 2016.

"Grant me chastity and continence (e.g. "sexual purity") but not yet. I was afraid you might hear my prayer quickly, and that you might too rapidly heal me of the disease of lust which I preferred to satisfy rather than suppress."[21]

Of course Augustine was speaking metaphorically of lust as a "disease" since it has symptoms *similar* to a "disease." It seems incurable – unless the Great Physician comes in His power. But are we tired of the sin yet? Do we *truly* want freedom from it? Or is it like the little red lizard in C. S. Lewis' *The Great Divorce*?

The lizard that was perched on the man's shoulder was a picture of lust and an angel had its hands around the lizard ready to put this sin to death once and for all. But the angel could not do so unless he had the man's permission. The man hemmed and hawed and rationalized his sin – *the lizard is sleeping; let's do this gradually it's not bothering me now; killing this sin will hurt me too much – in fact I may die if I don't have this in my life any longer...* Then finally, the man gives permission and the lizard is put to death.[22] How badly do we want this sin to be crushed and killed once and for all?

For the believer in Jesus Christ, there is hope. There is not futility or hopelessness or darkness or spiritual blindness. The little red lizard can indeed be killed. This is why we are urged to,*"be renewed in the spirit of your minds"* (Ephesians 4:23).[23]

---

[21] St. Augustine, *Confessions*, trans. Henry Chadwick (New York: Oxford University Press), Book 8, Chapter 7.17, 145.

[22] C. S. Lewis, *The Great Divorce* (New York: McMillan, 1946), 99-102.

[23] This is covered in more depth in my book, *"The Beauty of Biblical Meditation,"* available on www.Amazon.com

8) Pornography Turns Users into <u>Liars</u>

It usually surprises people when I tell them that those who are immersed in sexual sin are typically accomplished and compulsive liars. Why do they become liars? It's because they have made it a practice to deceive or outright lie about where they have been, what they have been doing, what Internet sites they have visited, etc. It also becomes more tempting to lie when there is fear over a spouse becoming upset. If a wife finds out that her husband is looking at pornography online, then she will understandably be upset.

And then she will interrogate him about why he would do such a thing to her? Doesn't he find her attractive anymore? She cannot compete with the images on the screen, so she becomes agitated at his disloyalty and his wandering eyes and lustful heart.

Her fears begin to drive her to worry and also drive her to anger and rage. The fear takes root and then she becomes bitter (Hebrews 12:14-15).

So rather than the husband having to experience all of the "drama" of a wife having a meltdown, he does what is easier and more convenient – he lies. And then he gets away with it, so he lies more. His own fears of getting caught lead him to lie. So fear grips her heart ("my husband doesn't love me") and fear grips his heart ("I might get caught" or "she'll yell and scream at me if I confess this to her").

And then when this happens he starts making lying into a habit – it becomes a regular practice. The lying becomes such a problem that he lies about just about anything – even mundane, non-sinful actions. It is probably no coincidence that Paul warns about "empty words" immediately after speaking about sexual sin (Ephesians 5:3-6).

9) Pornography is a "Private" Sin, not a "Public" one

If you have trouble with anger or taming your tongue, people will hear it and see it. It is obvious to all the people around you. If you become a drunkard, eventually the consequences will catch up with you. You will jeopardize your job and people will know that you struggle with alcohol. Alcohol can be smelled on your breath, or you will stagger home one day after a drunken spell or get a DUI while driving your car. The same is true for drugs. You may drive while intoxicated, or under the influence of a drug and have your license revoked, lose your job, etc. Worse yet, you may kill someone. But you won't kill anyone with pornography. Actually, that's not true. As I've been saying, you will murder your own soul. You yourself will inflict this upon your own soul, so pornography usage is a form of suicide of the soul. No one else is doing it to you. Pornography can be hidden for years – even decades if you have a spouse who is not suspicious of your activities, or if you have a spouse who is very trusting of you.

There will not be the obvious outward signs of this problem like there would be with drugs or alcohol.[24] This is why it is so deadly. It is a "private" sin that is performed solo, when no one else is around. And it's typically not a "group" activity like drinking and drugs. Many people are gripped by pornography and no one else knows about it, or even suspects it since it is an incognito sin. But though this man's ways are not known before the eyes of others, they are known before the eyes of the Lord.

---

[24] It should be noted, however, that a man's wife will eventually see patterns of behavior, mannerisms, even a certain "deadness" in her husband's eyes. that will give her evidence of her husband indulging in pornography. She will typically pick up on these signs when no one else will. I have had many wives tell me they "know" when their husband's are viewing pornography even when they don't have concrete evidence. Invariably they are proven right.

"For a man's ways are before the eyes of the Lord, and He ponders all his paths." (Proverbs 5:21).

10) With Pornography you "Reap What You Sow"[25]

One of the most well-known agricultural proverbs in Scripture is found in Galatians 6 and it applies to the man who is gripped by pornography and uses it to his own destruction.

"Do not be deceived: God is not mocked, for whatever one sows, that he will also reap. For the one who sows to his own flesh will from the flesh reap corruption, but the one who sows to the Spirit will from the Spirit reap eternal life." *(Galatians 6:7-8)*

Just as in agriculture, so in spiritual matters – God has designed us such that there is a direct correlation between sowing and reaping. If you sow corn, you will not reap tomatoes. If you sow potatoes, you will not reap wheat. Likewise, if you sow pornography, you will not reap a godly life.

If you only sow what is of "bodily interest," you will reap only the "here and now" of life's earthly pleasures.[26] In his previous chapter, Galatians 5:19, Paul has outlined how the "works of the flesh" produce "sexual immorality, impurity, and sensuality." This is obvious when it is referring to those indulged in pornography.

---

[25] Pure Life Ministries Email, *How Pornography is Affecting More than just You*, by Nate Danser, August 16, 2016.

[26] Leon Morris, *Galatians – Paul's Charter of Christian Freedom* (Downers Grove: InterVarsity, 1996), 182-183.

What is not quite as obvious is that many (most?) of the other works of the flesh will also be produced by the very same lust that is behind pornography.

God is not *mocked* about this. If you continue to indulge in pornography, the Holy Spirit cannot produce a godly man. God didn't make us that way and to say otherwise is to think we can somehow "trick" God. Eight different forms of anger are listed as "works of the flesh" in Galatians 5:20-21.[27] It is no coincidence that men & women who indulge in pornography often have trouble with anger. *Drunkenness and orgies (carousing, reveling, partying)* (5:21) often accompany pornography since these are all forms of escapism from life's perceived inequities.

Even the words previously mentioned (*impurity and sensuality*) can be viewed from another angle. For men who indulge in pornography, they may insist that their wives or girlfriends dress more provocatively and steer them away from more modest clothing. And for women who "commit" (see page 20) pornography, they may wear more revealing clothing so as to attract other men like the women in the porn video – and in the process attract the wrong kind of guys.

Since moral corruption is the result of such "sowing to the flesh," the consequences can show up in other ways that may seem unrelated but in actuality are directly connected. Daniel became so engrossed in pornography that he often skipped work, or went off to a corner office to view pornography. His job performance suffered so drastically that he nearly lost his job. Janet was moderately overweight and indulged in pornographic fantasies. She got depressed as she looked at the other firm bodies in the videos and compared them to her own. So in order to look like these women she developed eating disorders to lose more weight.

---

[27] "Enmity, strife, jealousy, fits of anger, rivalries, dissensions, divisions, and envy."

John was so gripped by pornography that he would not spend sufficient time on his college courses and in the process he was in danger of flunking out of school. Larry's employer had a strict code that the office computers were not to be used for inappropriate purposes. Even though Larry knew that pornography certainly qualified, he could only resist for so long – eventually he gave in – and promptly lost his job.

Ann had so regularly viewed pornography that she deliberately wore low cut dresses to show off her ample cleavage. And then she would delight in men whose eyes would fix on her deliberately revealed skin. Steven regularly took Viagra since it was nearly impossible for him to gain an erection with his wife. His wife was not unattractive or overweight, but Steven's years of sexual sin caused him to "need" the Viagra boost since his wife's middle-aged body certainly could not "compete" with young porn stars. There is very often a direct connection between men taking Viagra or Cialis and their indulgence in sexual sin – especially pornography. Eventually real life sex with their wives cannot compete with the fantasy so medication is required for them to perform and give them an artificial "boost." And then the wives feel demoralized and humiliated so this not only kills the sexual relationship but any romance that may have existed at one time between them. This is how marriages die.

What is most tragic is that these people do not see the gradual change that happened in their hearts that led to the deadly behaviors. But their friends could see these outward changes, yet they were totally unaware of pornography being behind it since it is so effectively hidden from plain view.

Chapter 3

The Power of the Holy Spirit to Overcome Pornography

One of the common problems men have with pornography is that many appear to lack the "power" to overcome this sin. It seems to grip them so tightly, that they appear to be incapable of conquering it. They try and try and have some level of success for a short period of time and yet fall right back into this over and over again. The pattern is common and so is the sense of hopelessness that accompanies it. I am convinced that many of the men whom I have counseled are absolutely sincere, yet they seem to be unable to access any spiritual strength to overcome this sin. They appear to be "powerless" to resist temptation. What is the root of this problem?

Power Comes From the Holy Spirit

Where do Christians get their "power" from? The universal testimony of the Scriptures is that it comes through the gospel by the Holy Spirit.

"But you will receive power when the Holy Spirit has come upon you, and you will be my witnesses in Jerusalem and in all Judea and Samaria and to the end of the earth." (Acts 1:8)

"May the God of hope fill you with all joy and peace in believing, so that by the power of the Holy Spirit you may abound in hope." (Romans 15:13)

"by the power of signs and wonders, by the power of the Spirit of God..." (Romans 15:19)

"For Christ did not send me to baptize but to preach the gospel, and not with words of eloquent wisdom, lest the cross of Christ be emptied of its power. For the word of the cross is folly to those who are perishing, but to us who are being saved it is the power of God." (1 Corinthians 1:17-18)

"(and) my speech and my message were not in plausible words of wisdom, but in demonstration of the Spirit and of power." (1 Corinthians 2:4)

"For the kingdom of God does not consist in talk but in power." (1 Corinthians 4:20)

"that according to the riches of His glory He may grant you to be strengthened with power through His Spirit in your inner being." (Ephesians 3:16)

"(because) our gospel came to you not only in word, but also in power and in the Holy Spirit and with full conviction." (1 Thessalonians 1:5)

"for God gave us a spirit not of fear but of power and love and self control." (2 Timothy 1:7)

"And Jesus returned in the power of the Spirit to Galilee..." (Luke 4:14)

"...God anointed Jesus of Nazareth with the Holy Spirit and with power..." (Acts 10:38)

The source of a Christian's "power" is the presence and the indwelling of the Spirit of God. And as we see above, the Spirit of God is connected with the good news of the gospel of Jesus Christ. The good news brings power because it does not come to a person separate from the Holy Spirit. Regeneration (being "born again") is a work of the Holy Spirit (John 3:5-8; Titus 3:4-6). This power to overcome sin does not come through "self effort," nor is it by "trying harder" that a believer will grow stronger. It is also not mere "words" ("I won't look at porn again"), nor good intentions ("This is a deadly sin – I have to stop"). There is no magic involved in overcoming the grip of pornography. It is not smoke and mirrors. It is only going to happen through the power of God. The unanimous testimony of the Word of God is that the Spirit of God is the source of this strength. The Holy Spirit "produces" this in the soul of man.

"But the fruit of the Spirit is love, joy, peace, patience, kindness, goodness, faithfulness, gentleness, self-control; against such things there is no law." (Galatians 5:22-23)

The production of this "fruit" is solely a work of the Holy Spirit. Perhaps the last fruit should be translated as "Spirit-controlled" rather than "self-controlled" so that we are not misled regarding "Who" gives this ability. The ability comes from Him, not from wishful thinking. Sexual sin, including "immorality, impurity, sensuality and orgies" comes from man's own efforts ("works of the flesh") and are devoid of the Holy Spirit's presence (Galatians 5:19-21). For those believers who minimize or marginalize the ministry of the Holy Spirit, they operate from a theological grid that is more "Binitarian" than "Trinitarian."

Being "Filled" With the Holy Spirit

The Scriptures teach that the Holy Spirit is "with you forever" (John 14:16) and that He "dwells with you and in you" (John 14:17; Romans 8:9-11). There is a deep work of God done in the heart of believers where God "fills" them with His Holy Spirit. We are urged to "be filled *with the Spirit*" (Ephesians 5:18). This imperative ("be filled") is not merely to be taken individually, but should be seen as the experience of the entire community of believers. It is "corporate" not only "individual" yet there is an individual sense to being filled with the Spirit. So this "filling" is not just for a select few, it is for all believers. It is likely that this thought in 5:18 is linked and connected back to Paul's words in Ephesians 3:16 &19. There he speaks not only of the "power" of the Holy Spirit (3:16 – "be strengthened with power through His Spirit in your inner being"), but also of being filled with the very presence of God by His Spirit ("be filled with all the fullness of God").[28] This is a fantastic blessing for God's people and is to be lived out by the local church through expressions of "speaking, singing, thanking and submitting" as can be seen by the participles in Ephesians 5:19-21. These grace-filled activities all evidence the presence of God in the soul.

Being filled with the Holy Spirit also appears to be something that "happens" to believers (Acts 2:4; 4:8; 7:55) and can come as a result of prayer (Acts 4:31). It is also a recognizable trait of some but not all believers (Acts 6:3, 5; 11:24; 13:9). But as we said above, all "can" and "should" be filled with the Holy Spirit. The filling of the Spirit can even be bestowed by laying on of hands (Acts 9:17). It is evident that there can be a connection between joy in the Lord and being filled with the Holy Spirit ("the disciples were filled with joy and with the Holy Spirit" - Acts 13:52).

---

[28] Gordon Fee, *God's Empowering Presence* (Peabody, MA: Hendrickson Publishers, 1994), 721-722.

Regarding those who persist in struggling with the grip of pornography, it can safely be concluded that they are *not* filled with the Holy Spirit. But let's consider this aspect of "joy" further since it seems to be such an important ingredient.

Joy and the Holy Spirit

Those who struggle with pornography are typically discontent with their lives. They wrestle with lust since they are longing for more than what they have at the moment. Pleasure is their goal, yet it is pleasure at the expense of the sanctification of their own souls. As we have seen above, being "filled" with the Holy Spirit results in a transformed life. Further study demonstrates that wherever "joy" is present, the Holy Spirit seems to likewise be present in the heart of that believer. Would this joy from the Holy Spirit satiate the discontented soul that seeks out pornographic pleasure?

"May the God of hope fill you with all joy and peace in believing, so that by the power of the Holy Spirit you may abound in hope." (Romans 15:13)

"And the disciples were filled with joy and with the Holy Spirit." (Acts 13:52)

"And when they came up out of the water, the Spirit of the Lord carried Philip away, and the eunuch saw him no more, and went on his way rejoicing." (Acts 8:39)

"And you became imitators of us and of the Lord, for you received the word in much affliction, with the joy of the Holy Spirit." (1 Thessalonians 1:6)

"But the fruit of the Spirit is love, joy, peace, patience, kindness, goodness, faithfulness, gentleness, self-control; against such things there is no law." (Galatians 5:22-23)

There is a deliberate contrast between the "fruit of the Spirit" that is described in Galatians 5:22-23 ("love, joy, peace, patience, kindness, goodness, faithfulness, gentleness, self-control") and the "works of the flesh" in Galatians 5:19-21 ("sexual immorality, impurity, sensuality, idolatry, etc."). Our "works" are those things that we do by our own strength and are the sinful impulses, which seek to gain control of the will.[29] But the term "fruit" is singular, implying that this is one united product of the Holy Spirit. You cannot produce this fruit by your own efforts or by trying to "be good." Additionally, however, these are a collective cluster of qualities that should be manifested in every believer.[30] So even though we are highlighting only "joy" here, the entirety of the virtues listed are to be descriptive of the saint who is indwelt by the Spirit of God. And this "joy" which the Holy Spirit produces will overcome the heart bent on sin. No amount of law or legalism will free someone from the grips of lust. Colossians 2:23 reminds us that all of our self efforts and best of intentions are of *"no value in stopping the indulgence of the flesh."* It is not that legalism does a "little" good, or that it is moderately helpful. Note that the Word of God tells us that it is of "no value" in freeing us. It is only going to happen through the presence of the Holy Spirit working in the soul of man. Those who are filled with the joy of the Holy Spirit will not pursue the momentary pleasures of lust in pornography. Therefore, we should *pursue* the presence and the power of the Holy Spirit.

---

[29] Charles R. Erdman, *The Epistle of Paul to the Galatians –An Exposition* (Philadelphia: Westminster Press, 1966), 117.

[30] Morris, *Galatians*, 173.

"How much more will the heavenly Father give the Holy Spirit to those who ask Him?" (Luke 11:13)

Our desires need to be holy desires. In fact, the Scriptures present this as a normal and expected part of the Christian life. If we scan the Word of God, we see frequent mention of longings, hungering, thirsting and yearning for God and holiness.

"Your name and remembrance are the desire of our soul. My soul yearns for You in the night; my spirit within me earnestly seeks You." (Isaiah 26:8-9)

"One thing I have asked of the Lord, that will I seek after: that I may dwell in the house of the Lord all the days of my life, to gaze upon the beauty of the Lord and to inquire in His temple." (Psalm 27:4)

"As a deer pants for flowing streams, so pants my soul for You, O God. My soul thirsts for God for the living God. When shall I come and appear before God?." (Psalm 42:1-2)

"O God, You are my God; earnestly I seek You; my soul thirsts for You; my flesh faints for You, as in a dry and weary land where there is no water. So I have looked upon You in the sanctuary, beholding Your power and glory." (Psalm 63:1-2)

"How lovely is Your dwelling place O Lord of hosts! My soul longs, yes, faints for the courts of the Lord; my heart and flesh sing for joy to the living God." (Psalm 84:1-2)

"My soul is consumed with longing for your rules at all times." (Psalm 119:20)

"Your testimonies are my delight; they are my counselors." (Psalm 119:24)

"I open my mouth and pant, because I long for your commandments." (Psalm 119:131)

"Whom have I in heaven but You? And there is nothing on earth that I desire besides You." (Psalm 73:25)

"I wait for the Lord, my soul waits, and in His word I hope; my soul waits for the Lord more than watchmen for the morning, more than watchmen for the morning." (Psalm 130:5-6)

"I stretch out my hands to You; my soul thirsts for You like a parched land. Answer me quickly O Lord! My spirit fails! Hide not Your face from me, lest I be like those who go down to the pit." (Psalm 143:6-7)

Jesus called such a man "blessed" who hungers and thirsts for righteousness – "Blessed are those who hunger and thirst for righteousness, for they shall be satisfied." (Matthew 5:6) and in the end of the age Jesus says, "To the thirsty I will give from the spring of the water of life without payment." (Revelation 21:6)[31]

As Jonathan Edwards aptly wrote:

"Our hungerings and thirstings after God and Jesus Christ and after holiness can't be too great for the value of these things, for they are things of infinite value. . . . [Therefore] endeavor to promote spiritual appetites by laying yourself in the way of allurement...There is no such thing as excess in our taking of this spiritual food. There is no such virtue as temperance in spiritual feasting."[32]

---

[31] Jonathan Edwards, *Religious Affections* (Ames, IA: International Outreach Online Edition, n.d.), 10.

[32] Jonathan Edwards, "The Spiritual Blessings of the Gospel Represented by a Feast" in *Sermons and Discourses*, 1723-1729, ed. Kenneth Minkema (New Haven, Conn.: Yale University Press, 1997), 286.

Quenching and Grieving the Holy Spirit

"*Do not quench the Spirit*" (1 Thessalonians 5:19 - ESV)

"*Do not extinguish the Spirit's fire*" (1 Thessalonians 5:19 – Berkeley Version)

We need to understand that we can also interfere with the ministry of the Holy Spirit within us. His work is often connected to "fire" (Matthew 3:11; Luke 3:16; 12:49; Acts 2:3-4; Romans 12:11) and to "quench" is to extinguish that fire that the Holy Spirit has lit in a man's heart (cf. Hebrews 11:34; Matthew 12:20). We quench the Spirit's work when we "smother" His presence within us.[33] When we walk in the flesh, according to our own will and our own desires rather than in a way that pleases the Spirit of God, we disinvite His work in our souls. We have to remember that He is the "Holy" Spirit, and when we consistently live in a manner that is not holy, He is treated as if He is not welcome in our hearts. We pour cold water on His burning, purifying presence within our souls.

"*And do not grieve the Holy Spirit of God by Whom you were sealed for the day of redemption.*" (Ephesians 4:30)

Likewise, we can bring "grief" to the Spirit of God. Think of what happens to your relationship with another person when you "grieve" them.

---

[33] Though I am not a fan of these Bible versions, the *Living Bible* translates this passage as "Do not smother the Holy Spirit." and the *New Living Translation* renders it, "Do not stifle the Holy Spirit."

If I grieve someone, do we get closer or do we drift further apart? Does that person want to be around me anymore? Does that person enjoy my presence or does he seek to avoid me? Although the Holy Spirit is certainly not hyper-sensitive like we can be, the analogy is an appropriate one – when we grieve Him, He is unwelcome.

We are sending Him a message loud and clear.

In the context of Ephesians 4, we grieve the Holy Spirit when we speak in a corrupt or anger-filled manner. Likewise if we indulge in immoral behavior, we grieve Him since He is Holy, and immorality is contrary to holiness.

If the Holy Spirit is the "power" within us, just the fact that we can quench or extinguish His work must be taken seriously. The fact that by our actions we can grieve Him should give us pause about how we live our lives. We must be wary of this danger since we are completely dependent upon the Spirit of God to live a God-glorifying Christian life. We can quench and grieve the Spirit of God in such a way that we become completely powerless and are reliant upon our own resources to battle against the temptations of life. The Holy Spirit is the source of a Christian's power and in the next chapter we will see how He gives this power to believers through grace.

Chapter 4

The Power of God's Grace in the Gospel

Even though the Spirit of God produces this joy that overcomes sin, all of us know that we often do not resist the pull of temptation. In fact, men gripped by pornography often describe themselves as "powerless" to resist these temptations. Surely that is how it "feels," yet that is part of the deception of the enemy and part of the delusion in our own souls. At times we are tempted to think that there is no point in resisting – "*resistance is futile.*" Most of the men I have counseled who have been gripped by pornography admit to me that, "a little porn is not enough." The pull of porn goes on and on and on for hours and hours. It's not like they view one or two videos and then they are finished. They feel helpless and compelled to sin over and over again.

But this lie tries to convince us that God's grace is not truly "abounding."

This work of the Holy Spirit is so powerful in the soul, that the Bible often describes saints as "abounding" in God's Grace. God doesn't give us "barely enough" help in order to live a godly life. It is not that we will just "get by" with the left-overs of His kindness. We have an abundance; an increasing amount; an overwhelming measure of this power of God that is working in our souls by the Spirit of God.

"Moreover the law entered that the offense might abound. But where sin abounded, <u>grace abounded much more</u>." (Romans 5:20, NKJV)

The grace that "abounded much more" is the key word here.[34] Paul deliberately uses a stronger word when describing what grace has done. But then he even puts a prefix on that stronger word to make the word into a superlative (we could say "superabounded"). Whatever sin did to us, grace did *far more* to us. Grace did not just nullify what sin did. Grace doesn't just cancel out what sin did. Grace doesn't just counteract what sin has done. Grace doesn't just balance the scales. Grace doesn't just give us a fighting chance.[35]

Grace has done *a lot more*. Grace has done *way more*. Grace has done *overwhelmingly more*. Grace has done *far, far more*. Paul doesn't have words to say it better, to say it fuller or to say it with more emphasis. If we were to write in the 21st century, perhaps we would <u>underline</u> the word, or we would make the word **bold**, or we would *italicize* the word, or put an exclamation point at the end! Maybe we would even put two exclamation points!! Or maybe we would <u>underline</u> and *italicize* and **bold** the word and put two exclamation points at the end!! I'm guessing you get the point by now. You cannot say "too much" about what has happened in our souls by God's truly amazing grace.

---

[34] Martyn Lloyd Jones, *Romans – An Exposition of Chapter 5 - Assurance* (Grand Rapids: Zondervan, 1971), 298-300.

[35] Jonathan Edwards, *The Power of God - A Jonathan Edwards Commentary on the Book of Romans,* edited and compiled by David S. Lovi and Benjamin Westerhoff (Eugene, OR: Pickwick Publications, 2013), 110.

Just looking at the book of Ephesians, we see the same things being said about this "superabounding" grace.

"His *glorious grace*" (Ephesians 1:6)

"*the riches of His grace which He lavished upon us*" (Ephesians 1:7-8)

"*the immeasurable greatness of His power toward us who believe.*" (Ephesians 1:19)

"*the immeasurable riches of His grace*" (Ephesians 2:7)

"*the unsearchable riches of Christ*" (Ephesians 3:8)

"*Now to Him who is able to do far more abundantly than all we ask or think, according to the power at work within us.*" (Ephesians 3:20)

And we should note that both in Romans 5:20 and also here in Ephesians 3:20, this grace of God that is described is not merely an abstract or theological thought. In other words, it is not "some Christians have this and some do not." Paul says in Ephesians 3:20 that this "far more abundant" grace is "according to the power at work within us." It is *already* at work within His people.[36]

"*And God is able to make all grace abound to you...*" (2 Corinthians 9:8)

---

[36] Hendriksen, *Ephesians*, 175.

If we pick up where we left off in Romans 5, we will discover more about the unparalleled power of God's abounding grace.

"so that, as sin reigned in death, <u>grace might also reign</u> through righteousness leading to eternal life through Jesus Christ our Lord." (Romans 5:21)

The man who is gripped by pornography feels as if this sin dominates his life more than anything else. It compels him to fulfill his lusts. It rules over his soul. As Paul describes it here "sin reign(s) in death." Pornography is a murderer. But it is not just pornography that murders the soul and brings spiritual and physical death. All sin does that. This is the point that is being made in Romans 5. We all died in Adam (Romans 5:12-14) and because of this, we are all *born* under the dominion of sin. Whether you were born to godly parents, or the most depraved parents in history, you were born like this and you cannot escape this - except through the gospel of Jesus Christ. And now because the grace of the gospel is so very powerful, so abounding in grace, now this grace "reigns" in the soul of the saint. This grace far exceeds the power of sin. It <u>far</u> exceeds it.

To say that God's grace "reigns" in us is yet another way to describe the "abounding grace." This is what Paul has been doing throughout the entirety of Romans 5. If you notice, Paul has been speaking about the "much more" aspect of this work of God in our souls on numerous other occasions in the fifth chapter of Romans:

"Since therefore, we have now been justified by His blood, <u>much more</u> shall we be saved by Him from the wrath of God." (Romans 5:9)

"For if while we were enemies we were reconciled to God by the death of His Son, <u>much more</u> now that we are reconciled, shall we be saved by His life." (Romans 5:10)

"<u>More than that</u>, we also rejoice in God through our Lord Jesus Christ, through Whom we have now received reconciliation." (Romans 5:11)

"But the free gift is not like the trespass. For if many died through one man's trespass, <u>much more</u> have the grace of God and the free gift by the grace of that one man Jesus Christ <u>abounded for many</u>." (Romans 5:15)

"For if, because of one man's trespass, death reigned through that one man, <u>much more</u> will those who receive the <u>abundance of grace</u> and the free gift of righteousness reign in life through the one man Jesus Christ." (Romans 5:17)

It is crucial for us to grasp why God's grace is "much more" than our struggles. Every saint has tremendous power working in his soul solely due to the gospel. Brother (or sister), let these rich, biblical truths about the power of God's grace build and deepen your <u>faith</u>! Note the frequent description of "grace" as being associated with "God's power."

"My <u>grace</u> is sufficient for you, for my <u>power</u> is made perfect in weakness..." (2 Corinthians 12:9)

"Be <u>strengthened</u> by the <u>grace</u> that is in Christ Jesus..." (2 Timothy 2:1)

"And with <u>great power</u> the apostles ...and <u>great grace</u> was upon them." (Acts 4:33)

"And Stephen, <u>full of grace and power</u>, was doing great wonders and signs..." (Acts 6:8)

"Of this gospel I was made a minister according to the gift of God's <u>grace</u>, which was given me by the working of His <u>power</u>." (Ephesians 3:7)

This grace that reigns in us shows us the immeasurable strength and power that is given to us as His people. This should not only encourage and comfort us, but it also should be something we remind ourselves about when we wrestle with sin. Remember that "grace" by its very definition is undeserved and unearned. Grace is not just given to "good" Christians, but also to ones who feel as if they constantly fail. So if you are currently struggling with the temptations of pornography, God is giving you this "abounding" grace, just like He is giving it to your friend who doesn't struggle like you do (but remember that your friend struggles with "some" type of sin).

One of my favorite songs is by the group "Mercy Me" on their album "Lifer." The song is called *"Best News Ever"* and it reminds us that the gospel *"is not good news, it's the best news ever!"* When we realize that God's grace is "abounding all the more" towards us, how could we not see the gospel as "the best news ever"?

Chapter 5

The Slavery of Idolatry

Often I hear men tell me, "I wish God would keep me from pornography. *I cannot stop viewing it!*" But this is severely wrong headed and ultimately is simply an excuse to continue in sin. This is akin to saying, "*I have no choice. I have to sin.*" but once again this is a deception. They act as if this sin has "enslaved them," but in reality it is a self-imposed, voluntary slavery.[37] Though it is true that there is free and full forgiveness through the gospel of Jesus Christ, it is not true that Jesus will obey for us.

The commands in Scripture are there for a reason. And when God commands our obedience it is not only something we "should" do, but also something we "can" do.[38] And we "can" do this solely due to the abounding grace of God that is operating in our hearts. But remember that "superabounding" grace IS indeed powerfully reigning in your heart already.

---

[37] Ed Welch, "Just One More" – When Desires Don't Take No for an Answer (Phillipsburg, NJ: P & R Publishing, 2002), 14-15.

[38] Martyn Lloyd Jones, *Romans – An Exposition of Chapter 6 – The New Man* (Grand Rapids: Zondervan, 1972), 259.

The man who believes he "cannot" resist pornography has allowed idolatry to control him. Can a saint be gripped by an idol? According to Scripture, the answer is "yes"

"Do not be idolaters as some of them were..." (1 Corinthians 10:7)

"Therefore my beloved, flee from idolatry." (1 Corinthians 10:14)

"Little children, keep yourselves from idols." (1 John 5:21)

Scripture would not warn us about the dangers if it were not possible to be tempted into this sin. What is the connection between "idolatry" and "pornography"? In both the Old Testament (OT) and the New Testament (NT), there is an intimate connection between idolatry and sexual sin.

The book of Ezekiel speaks more about idols than any other book in Scripture. He uses a form of the word "idol" 46 times. In many of those instances, idolatry is connected to sexual sin:

6:9 - (*"whoring after their idols"*)

16:36 - (*"your lust was poured out...with all your abominable idols"*)

20:7 - (*"things your eyes feast on..with the idols"*)

23:30 - (*"you played the whore with...idols"*)

23:37 - (*"with their idols they have committed adultery"*)

37:23 - (*"defile themselves...with their idols"*)

Some scholars believe Ezekiel compared "idolatry" with "dung pellets" since the two Hebrew words are so intimately related to one another.[39] It was a term of derision that was intended to mock the foolishness and darkness of this particular sin.

Another way to view idolatry is to see how Ezekiel addresses the idolatry practiced among God's people. These words were given to Israel during the time of the Babylonian exile and it is certain that they have been *"infected by their Babylonian environment and the attractions of its idolatrous religion."*[40] This is similar to our surrounding culture today, which freely and ubiquitously promotes sexual titillation through pornographic video and photography. Our current brand of idolatry can be just as invasive to the human soul. In fact, Ezekiel uses a unique phrase three times to describe these elders of Israel – they *"took their idols into their hearts"* (Ezekiel 14:3, 4 & 7). This phrase "means to allow anything to come into the mind, to permit it to rise up in the heart, to be mentally busy therewith."[41] This is a reminder that idolatry is not merely an external act, but begins internally. It is one thing to set an idol on a table in the house, but it is quite another thing to have that idol *rule* in the heart. If it just sits on a shelf, it has little power.

---

[39] "Idolatry," in *New Bible Dictionary* 2nd Edition, ed. by J.D. Douglas, F.F. Bruce, J.I. Packer, N. Hillyer, D. Guthrie, A.R. Millard, D.J. Wiseman (Wheaton, IL: Tyndale House, 1962), 505 and "Idolatry," in *International Standard Bible Encyclopedia,* Vol. 2, - E-J, ed. by Geoffrey W. Bromiley, Everett F. Harrison, Roland K. Harrison, William Sanford LaSor, Lawrence T. Geraty, Edgar W. Smith Jr. (Grand Rapids: Eerdmans, 1982), 796. Also see Francis Brown, S. R. Driver, Charles A. Briggs, *The New Brown-Driver-Briggs-Gesenius Hebrew and English Lexicon,* (Peabody, MA: Hendrickson Publishers, 1979), "Galal," entry 1557, 165.

[40] John B. Taylor, *Ezekiel – An Introduction and Commentary* (Downers Grove: InterVarsity, 1969), 126.

[41] C.F. Keil and F. Delitzsch, *Commentary on the Old Testament, Volume 9 – Ezekiel, Daniel,* (Grand Rapids: Eerdmans, 1986 reprinted), 178.

But when the idol is "taken" into the heart, it has influence, it controls, and it makes demands. It affects desire and inflames it. It will not take "no" for an answer. The idol that is taken into the heart strikes at the seat of desire and enthrones self. It strategically subverts God's supremacy and God's rule and makes His Lordship of no account.[42]

The foolishness of idolatry is aptly portrayed in Psalm 115:8

"Those who make them (idols) become like them; so do all who trust in them."

Just like Roman Catholic worship[43] of relics demonstrates the folly of their idolatry, so does the man who takes the idol of pornography into his own heart. Catholics plunge into extreme and irrational folly when they worship the bones of the Apostle Peter, the joint of a finger of the Apostle Thomas, the tongue of St. Anthony of Padua and even the mummified head of St. Catherine of Siena.[44]

---

[42] Patrick Fairbairn, *Commentary on Ezekiel* (Grand Rapids: Kregel, 1989 reprint), 153.

[43] Catholics make the claim that they do not "worship" but only "venerate" these relics since they claim these "draw them closer to God." But this is a dubious argument since the words are interchangeable and basically are synonymous. Peter, Paul, Barnabas and even the angel who gave John the book of Revelation all refused veneration/worship (Acts 10:25-26; 14:15; Revelation 19:10; 22:8-9) and so would any saint whether he was dead or alive. Needless to say, Catholics practice idolatry when they worship/ venerate relics, just as they do when the pray to Mary and the saints.

[44] See for instance, www.theguardian.com/artanddesign/jonathanjones-blog/2013/nov/18/st-peters-bones-christian-relics accessed on 8/11/17.

Why would someone embrace such grotesque absurdities? Likewise, with pornography God, "gives them over to a debased mind" (Romans 1:28) so that they are blind to their own depravity.

Enslavement to the idol ensues as men "set the stumbling block of their iniquity before their faces." (Ezekiel 14:3). This means that it is "a thing which a man will not put out of his mind."[45] This is precisely what happens with the idolatrous pornographic image - a man will not put it out of his mind and as a consequence it not only consumes him, but pulls him away from God.

This is why God does not take idolatry lightly but instead urges the man to "repent and turn away from your idols" (Ezekiel 14:6). Another vivid example is seen in Ezekiel 20:7, "things your eyes feast on…with idols"). Men "feast their eyes" upon the pornographic photo or video and "take the idol (the image/video) into their hearts." This is breaking the first of the 10 commandments ("You shall have not other gods before Me" – Exodus 20:3). Furthermore, when pornography is taken into the heart like an idol, it remains underground and hidden.[46] If someone bowed down to a statue out in the open, it would be obvious to all regarding which god was worshipped. Since pornography is viewed in secret, the idolatry can easily be cloaked and concealed in secret. A person can externally maintain the confessions of his faith and participate in worship services in his church yet all the while he has a secret idol that no one sees and no one suspects. It is no wonder that many men feel powerless over their idol of pornography. It maintains a hidden grasp on their souls. And since it is hidden, other believers cannot help them since they do not know about the struggle.

---

[45] Keil & Delitzsch, *Ezekiel*, 178.

[46] Tripp, *Instruments in the Redeemer's Hands*, 67.

The slavery of idolatry is not only seen in the Old Testament (OT) but also we see the combination of "idolatry" and "sexual immorality" linked together in every sin list that Paul gives us in the New Testament (NT):

Galatians 5:19-20 – "*the works of the flesh are evident: sexual immorality...idolatry*"

1 Corinthians 5:11 – "*not to associate with anyone...guilty of sexual immorality or greed, or is an idolater*"

Ephesians 5:5 – "*everyone who is sexually immoral or impure, or who is covetous (that is an idolater)*"

Colossians 3:5 – "*Put to death...sexual immorality...and covetousness, which is idolatry*"[47]

There are also additional occurrences of "idolatry" and "sexual immorality" in other passages of Scripture in both the OT and the NT:

"*Do not be idolaters as some of them were...we must not indulge in sexual immorality*" (1 Corinthians 10:7-8)

"*the people began to whore with the daughters of Moab. These invited the people to the sacrifice of their gods...*" (Numbers 25:1-2)

"*so that they might eat food sacrificed to idols and practice sexual immorality...*" (Revelation 2:14)

---

[47] *New Bible Dictionary*, p. 505.

"On a high and lofty mountain you have set your bed, and there you went up to offer sacrifice…you have made a covenant for yourself with them, you have loved their bed, you have looked on nakedness." (Isaiah 57:7-8)

"My people inquire of a piece of wood, and their walking staff gives them oracles. For a spirit of whoredom has led them astray, and they have left their God to play the whore…your daughters play the whore, and your brides commit adultery…the men themselves go aside with prostitutes and sacrifice with cult prostitutes" (Hosea 4:12-14)

"…teaching and seducing my servants to practice sexual immorality and to eat food sacrificed to idols.." (Revelation 2:20)

"the sexually immoral, sorcerers, idolaters…" (Revelation 21:8)

In Romans 1:18-32 idolatry is displayed through the sexual immorality that was rampant in Rome at the time. The idolatry of pornography, like other sexual sin is due to an excessive devotion to the self and is borne of deep pride in the heart.[48] If a man will not humble himself, he will continue to think too highly of himself and in his mind have a "right" to pornographic viewing. Pride is closely associated with lust as in 1 John 2:16

"For all that is in the world – the lust of the flesh and the lust of the eyes and the boastful pride of life, is not from the Father, but is from the world." (1 John 2:16, NASB Updated Edition)

The pride connected with indulging in pornography is "an attitude of being dissatisfied with what one has or is."[49]

This can be deadly to the man who continually chooses not to turn away from his sin:

---

[48] *International Standard Bible Encyclopedia*, Vol. Two, pp. 799-800.

[49] Steve Gallagher, *i The Root of Sin Exposed* (Dry Ridge, KY: Pure Life Ministries, 2017), 109.

"He who is often reproved, yet stiffens his neck, will suddenly be broken beyond healing." (Proverbs 29:1)

"The Lord tears down the house of the proud." (Proverbs 15:25)

"Whoever has a haughty look and an arrogant heart I will not endure." (Psalm 101:5b)

"The way of a fool is right in his own eyes, but a wise man listens to advice" (Proverbs 12:15)

"There are those who are clean in their own eyes but are not washed of their filth" (Proverbs 30:12)

"When pride comes, then comes disgrace, but with the humble is wisdom." (Proverbs 11:2)

"Pride goes before destruction, and a haughty spirit before a fall." (Proverbs 16:18)

"For where jealousy and selfish ambition exist, there will be disorder and every vile practice. But the wisdom from above is first pure..." (James 3:16-17a)

The priority must "first" be upon "purity" for a man to walk in wisdom before the Lord. The connection between sexual immorality, covetousness and idolatry helps us see how substituting sexual immorality for the grace of God drives the soul away from being "satisfied with God's goodness" (Jeremiah 31:14). This plunges the soul into idolatry. This is true whether it be adultery, fornication, pornography or other forms of sexual sin. Idolatry is the preoccupation of one's thinking that leads to *demanding* any temporal pleasure to gratify yourself.[50] The man's focus on "self" is at the root of his idolatry and the more self-centered the man is, the more he practices self-gratification.[51]

---

[50] Mark Shaw, *The Heart of Addiction* (Bemidji, MN: Focus Publishing, 2008), 77.

[51] Steve Gallagher, *At the Altar of Sexual Idolatry* (Dry Ridge, KY: Pure Life Ministries, 2007), 106-107.

Chapter 6

The Reality of Spiritual Warfare

Another reason that believers feel powerless in the face of pornography is due to the work of the enemy of our souls. Before we delve into this area, we should address something even more elementary. Most of us probably fall into one of two errors regarding the works of the devil.

C.S. Lewis once wrote:

"There are two equal and opposite errors into which our race can fall about the devils. One is to disbelieve in their existence. The other is to believe, and to feel an excessive and unhealthy interest in them. They themselves are equally pleased by both errors."[52]

I have no idea whether you the reader, "disbelieve" in the devil or if you have an "unhealthy interest" in him. Some of you reading this are probably too dismissive of the devil. You function without any conscious thought of demons wreaking havoc on humanity. Others of you reading this are so demon-centered that you see a demon behind every bush. I remember counseling one man who said he was "too educated" to believe in demons.

---

[52] Lewis, *The Screwtape Letters*, 3

I reminded him that he is not wiser than Jesus – who readily believed in them. If Jesus believed in them, then so should we.

On the other end, I remember reading about a woman who believed she had to cast demons out of her toaster in order for it to work. It would seem that C.S. Lewis was right - the devil loves either extreme. I would just ask you to have an open mind about this area since you may not be quite as "balanced" in this area as you believe you are. Don't assume that "all other Christians" besides you, are either too quick to believe in demons, or too quick to deny their involvement in the world. As Lewis warned, you don't want to "please" the devil with your mistaken theology. You may be tempted to think that you yourself are the one who is perfectly "balanced" in what you believe and everyone else is out of balance!

Even if we do believe in the devil's existence, we still may not believe he can do much to us. When we minimize the reality of spiritual warfare it is usually a symptom of something deeper that is out of order in our souls. Prayer and worship are often more ritual than relational. God's power is not sought and therefore very little is expected. The Bible becomes a rulebook to follow rather than the "Word" or "Voice" of the Living God. Sin is not seen as warfare on the soul, but rather as tweaks and adjustments that need to be made in life.[53]

We are talking about an all-out war, when we are speaking of spiritual warfare. It is *war*fare, not *peace*fare. This will not be won by light measures. It is not "like" a war; it "is" a war. This is not a time of peace; it's a time for battle – battle for your very soul. It is the "violent take it by force" (Matthew 11:12). You are not wrestling with a "disease" you are wrestling with the living breathing enemy of your soul.

---

[53] David Powlison, *Power Encounters – Reclaiming Spiritual Warfare* (Grand Rapids: Baker, 1995), 24.

"...we do not wrestle against flesh and blood, but against the rulers, against the authorities, against the cosmic powers over this present darkness, against the spiritual forces of evil in the heavenly places." (Ephesians 6:12)

One of the ways that the devil makes war against us is through his powers of "deception." Consider the following Scriptures, which identify this trait in him:

The Devil is a "Deceiver"

"...(the serpent said to the woman) did God actually say..." (Genesis 3:1)

"...so that we would not be <u>outwitted</u> by Satan; for we are not ignorant of his <u>designs</u>." (2 Corinthians 2:11)

"Put on the whole armor of God, that you may be able to stand against the <u>schemes</u> of the devil. For we do not wrestle against flesh and blood..." (Ephesians 6:11-12a)

"He (the devil) was a murderer from the beginning, and does not stand in the truth, because there is no truth in him. <u>When he lies he speaks out of his own character, for he is a liar and the father of lies</u>." (John 8:44)

"...Satan, the <u>deceiver</u> of the whole world..." (Revelation 12:9)

"(the beast who is empowered by Satan) <u>deceives</u> those who dwell on earth..." (Revelation 13:14)

"...so that he (Satan) might not <u>deceive</u> the nations any longer..." (Revelation 20:3)

"and the devil who had <u>deceived</u> them was thrown into the lake of fire..." (Revelation 20:10)

What are some of the ways that he can "deceive" you in regards to viewing pornographic photos and videos? The following are some examples of what he might impress upon your mind:

"A little porn won't hurt you"

"What happens in *Vegas, stays in Vegas"*

"Porn is not as bad as outright adultery, so therefore it is okay"

"No one else knows about this sin, so it's not hurting anyone"

"Everybody else looks at porn, so you might as well do it too"

"Those people who tell you they don't look at porn are lying – they are looking at it just as much as you are."

"This isn't "really" porn, it's just appreciating the human body"

"What you are looking at isn't as bad as the porn that other people look at – so it's okay"

"Getting your wife to view porn along with you will help your sex life – she'll be more interested in sex if you get her to look at it too"

"Viewing porn will prevent you from actually committing adultery with another woman, so therefore it is actually a good thing."

This is only a small sampling of what men have told me whom I have counseled. Our ability to rationalize and justify our sin is uncanny. And the devil is a master at helping us to do exactly that.

"For first there comes to the mind a bare thought of evil, then a strong imagination thereof, afterwards delight, and an evil motion, and then consent. And so by little and little our wicked enemy gets complete entrance, whilst he is not resisted in the beginning. And the longer a man is negligent in resisting, so much the weaker does he become daily in himself, and the enemy stronger against him."[54]

This is why we are called to "radical amputation" in regards to our sin.[55] Jay Adams coined this phrase in speaking of taking drastic measures to deal with our sin. We must not "play nice" with sin, but instead realize that radical measures will need to be taken. He bases this on the words of Jesus:

"If your right eye causes you to sin, tear it out and throw it away. For it is better that you lose one of your members than that your whole body be thrown into hell. And if your right hand causes you to sin, cut it off and throw it away. For it is better that you lose one of your members than that your whole body go into hell." (Matthew 5:29-30)

Obviously Jesus is using hyperbolic (exaggerated) language here to ensure that we do not miss the point of His teaching. He is not saying to literally cut off limbs or pluck out eyeballs. But you need to take drastic measures – if necessary – to deal with sins like pornography that you cannot overcome. The devil will use these as access points to tempt your soul if you do not put them to death. So you want to give him less ammunition that he can use against you.

You may need to change the friends you hang around with, the things you view on the Internet or certain movies or TV shows.

---

[54] Thomas a Kempis, *Of the Imitation of Christ*, (originally published 1418-1427; reprint Springdale: Whitaker House, 1981), 30.

[55] Jay Adams, *More Than Redemption – A Theology of Christian Counseling* (Phillipsburg, NJ: P & R Publishing, 1979), 263-266.

You may need to stay away from stores that openly display sexually oriented clothing, stay away from reading "romance novels" that are really just "soft porn" (women are especially susceptible here).

You may need to get rid of Internet access altogether, or go back to a flip phone rather than your smart phone that can access the Internet, or put a porn filter like "Covenant Eyes" on your computer, iPad and iPhone. I have counseled some men to change their jobs not because the job itself was evil, but because the temptations built into their work made it literally impossible to function without being exposed to things that would tempt them.

There is a lot that can be done here, but you have to decide whether you are at war or fooling yourself into thinking you are living in peace and porn is "no big deal." What I am suggesting here is not a new brand of legalism, but living in wisdom to protect your own soul.

"Fight the good fight of the faith. Take hold of the eternal life to which you were called and about which you made the good confession in the presence of many witnesses." (1 Timothy 6:12)

"Flee youthful passions and pursue righteousness, faith, love, and peace along with those who call on the Lord from a pure heart." (2 Timothy 2:22)

Fighting is generally wrong and could be dangerous and harmful to others. But there is one kind of fighting that God endorses. It is even called the "good" fight. Fight to maintain your faith. This does not mean "fight to continue to believe (for instance) in justification by faith," but more than likely it means "fight to continue to put your trust in God." You will be tempted to not believe that God is with you. You will be tempted to think that God has abandoned you. You will be tempted to NOT believe that *"He who is in you, is greater than he who is in the world"* (1 John 4:4). But don't allow your soul to be tempted away from biblical truth.

We need to remember that the devil and his demons do not "cause" anyone to sin. They may "tempt" us to sin, but they can never force us against our own will to sin against God. He can use your existing sin to tempt you into yet more sin. But you cannot blame the devil for your sin anymore than you can blame another human being. You are responsible and you need to be held accountable. God did not allow Eve to escape her sin because, "the devil made me do it" (Genesis 3:13), so neither can you. But one of the devil's strategies is to try to tempt us to sin.

The Devil is a "Tempter"

"Then Jesus was led up by the Spirit into the wilderness to be tempted by the devil...And the tempter came and said to Him (Jesus)..." (Matthew 4:1-3)

"And He (Jesus) was in the wilderness 40 days, being tempted by Satan." (Mark 1:13)

"(Satan said) Have You (God) not put a hedge around him and his house and all that he has, on every side? You have blessed the work of his hands, and his possessions have increased in the land. But stretch out Your hand and touch all that he has, and he will curse you to Your face." (Job 1:10-11)

"Then Satan answered the Lord and said, 'Skin for skin! All that a man has he will give for his life. But stretch out your hand and touch his bone and his flesh, and he will curse you to your face" (Job 2:4-5)

64

"Then Satan stood against Israel and incited David to number Israel." (1 Chronicles 21:1)

"Be sober-minded; be watchful. Your adversary the devil prowls around like a roaring lion, seeking someone to devour. Resist him, firm in your faith..." (1 Peter 5:8-9)

"Submit yourselves therefore to God. Resist the devil, and he will flee from you. Draw near to God, and He will draw near to you." (James 4:7-8)

The devil's one main goal in tempting you is to draw you into sin. He is capable of tempting your mind to believe something that is not true. When he tempted Jesus, he may have said something like, *"You are the Son of God Who created all things for Your own pleasure! But now You must be fiercely hungry due to fasting for 40 days. Why deprive Yourself – all things should serve YOU!" Satiate that hunger by turning these stones into bread – it's easy for YOU to do! It's just not right for you to suffer."* (Matthew 4:3). To David, he may have said, *"You yourself O mighty king have won so many battles. There is no king like you nor will there ever be. Just look at all the mighty warriors you have secured to build your majestic kingdom. Oh, if only you knew just how many men are loyal to you, it would surely glorify God and show the glory of the kingdom you have built."* (1 Chronicles 21:1-8). King David did fall as a result of the devil's temptation, but the Son of David did not.

A masterful work on spiritual warfare is "Precious Remedies Against Satan's Devices" by the Puritan Thomas Brooks. I'd urge you to get a copy of this thorough work on this important topic. In it, he lists twelve "devices" that the devil uses to afflict our souls and draw us into sin.

His premise originates in 2 Corinthians 2:11

"so that we would not be outwitted by Satan; for we are not ignorant of his designs (devices)."

We note that it is possible for the devil to "outwit" us and thus take advantage of us if our hearts become hardened in sin. His "devices" or "designs" – note the plural – are particularly sinister and speak of his plots, wiles, machinations, strategies and evil schemings.[56] In Ephesians 6:11 Scripture similarly speaks of the devil's "schemes." This is the treacherous work of the enemy that attempts to ambush the unsuspecting Christian much like the cunning tactics used by an army in wartime.[57] These traps are purposeful and crafty and are set to take prey while they are unaware of their impending doom. Sometimes Satan can trap us more easily by being clothed in sheep's skin than as a wolf. I once had an encounter with an actual KGB agent during a missions trip to a Soviet bloc country. Of course, I didn't know he was with the KGB until *after* my encounter with him. He was the friendliest, kindest, warm-hearted man I ever met – or so he seemed.

He was complimentary of my teaching of the Bible, spoke glowingly about our American President, and gave me a big Russian hug. He wanted his picture taken with me and I obliged. And then he started speaking very poorly about his own country's President. And then came the (devil's) hook – "What do YOU think of our country and our President? I wish we had a President like your American President!" I am so grateful that the Holy Spirit gave me wisdom at that very moment (Luke 12:12) and I said to him, "I don't know much about your President or your country, but I do love to talk about the gospel of Jesus Christ." I figured that if I was going to be imprisoned it would be better to do so for the sake of the gospel than for the sake of my political beliefs.

---

[56] Philip Edgcumbe Hughes, *Paul's Second Epistle to the Corinthians* (Grand Rapids: Eerdmans, 1962), 72.

[57] Thomas Brooks, *Precious Remedies Against Satan's Devices* (originally published 1652; reprint Wilmington, DE: Sovereign Grace Publishers, 1972), 11.

Nothing further happened, but it does illustrate how the devil often works – through flattery, an appearance of kindness, subterfuge, and not making his agenda known until it is too late.

Some of the 12 "devices" that Brooks examines[58] will be helpful in seeing how the enemy can effectively ensnare someone in pornographic sin:

1) <u>By Presenting the Bait While Hiding the Hook</u> > He will present the sweet, pleasant nature of the sin all the while hiding the poison and misery that will follow. Men are enticed by the lure of pornographic images and video since it excites not only his lusts, but also the imagination of what it would be like to be with someone like this. Satan puts out the bait and the unsuspecting prey takes the bait fully into his soul - and kills his own soul without him thinking about the consequences.

2) <u>By Making Light of the Sin</u> > *"It's just a "little" porn; there are others who do much more than you do. You can commit this sin without any danger to yourself. Surely it will not kill your soul."* This is how the devil draws us with a "lesser" sin and then step by step draws us into deeper and more deadly sins. One day it is a few clicks on porn sites, the next day, it is an hour long marathon of depraved viewing. One day it is pornography, the next day it is coldness to your wife. One day it is video porn, the next day it is cheating on your wife with another woman. Lust never says "enough" (Proverbs 30:15-16). Remember that, "a little leaven leavens the whole lump" (1 Corinthians 5:6).

3) <u>By Presenting God as Being Only Mercy</u> > *"Do not fear the sin of pornography, you will be forgiven because God is ready to show you mercy."* We forget that God *"(gives) them over to their stubborn hearts, to follow their own counsels."* (Psalm 81:12). We must remember

---

[58] Brooks, 12-61.

that God is indeed merciful, but He is also "just" as when He not only showed mercy to humanity but also justly poured out His wrath upon Jesus for our sin (Matthew 27:46). Recall that *"the steadfast love of the Lord is from everlasting to everlasting on those who fear Him."* (Psalm 103:17). The man gripped by porn is not fearing God. We are more like Satan than Saints when we argue from mercy to sinful liberty – *"continue in sin that grace may abound? May it never be!"* (Romans 6:1-2).

4) <u>By Giving the Impression that Repentance is Easy</u> > *"So what if you sin? You can turn from this tomorrow. You can confess, be sorrowful and ask forgiveness and all will be well again."* This view severely misunderstands how difficult it is to break with sin once it has settled in the heart. Repentance is not simply a work to be mustered up by man, but instead God must *"grant them repentance"* (2 Timothy 2:25). No man can demand that God "grant" him repentance since "to grant" is "to gift." Repentance is not only a turning from all sin, but also a "turning to all good; to a love of good, to a prizing of good, and to a following after all good."[59] It is not only hating our sin, but also hating ourselves for falling into the sin (*"therefore I despise myself and repent in dust and ashes."* Job 42:6).[60] And repentance is not a simple "one-time act" but instead is a continuous ongoing act that comes from a changed heart. Repentance is graphically described by Brooks as the "vomit of the soul."[61]

---

[59] Brooks, 33.

[60] Note here that Job does not attempt to "boost his self-esteem" ("I'm not a bad guy – why is everyone picking on me?"). Instead he humbles himself even though God Himself said Job had "spoken right of Me" (42:7-8). Typically our desire for more self-esteem is a sinful display of self-pity.

[61] Brooks, 36.

We should note that we can indeed "resist" the temptations that the devil hurls at us. Not only did Jesus do this, but both Peter and James urge this restraint upon believers as well. So when the devil tempts you to view pornography, know for certain that you can indeed resist due to the grace God gives every man.

"Submit yourselves therefore to God. Resist the devil, and he will flee from you." (James 4:7)

"Be sober-minded; be watchful. Your adversary the devil prowls around like a roaring lion, seeking someone to devour. Resist him, firm in your faith..." (1 Peter 5:8-9)

Do James and Peter urge us to resist "something" (a trial or a problem) or do they urge us to resist "someone" (the devil)? We are told that we can and must resist the devil, who is on the prowl and seeking to "devour us." He wants to "devour" your faith, your trust, your hope, your confidence in God's Truth.

He wants to draw you into temptation. He wants to see you fall. He wants to see you give in. He is trying to convince you that you "cannot" resist. After all, how do you resist someone whom you cannot see, cannot touch, cannot hear, and cannot even smell? The devil is not visible, yet you are supposed to "resist him."

How do you do that? Peter actually answers the question – *"Resist him – firm in your faith..."* (1 Peter 5:9). You resist the devil by *believing* what God has said. You resist him by *trusting* in God's Word. You resist him by *holding fast* to the truth. You won't be able to resist if you fight like an ordinary man would – get tough, bear down, empower yourself. No, those are "weapons of the flesh" and they will all fail you. Instead we fight with "divine power" and cling to the truth of the good news of the gospel and take our thoughts captive to obey Jesus (2

Corinthians 10:3-4). Plus remember, *"The Lord knows how to rescue the godly from trials (temptations)."* (2 Peter 2:9). The devil will actually <u>urge you</u> to fight this sin - as long as you fight it in the flesh. Remember he is not only a liar but also the *"father of lies"* (John 8:44).

He is even lying to you when you think that merely being tempted in itself is a sin. Jesus was tempted *in all ways* as we are, yet He did not sin. If being tempted was sinful, then Jesus Himself sinned. But we know He did NOT:

"For we do not have a high priest who is unable to sympathize with our weaknesses, but one who <u>in every respect has been tempted as we are, yet without sin.</u>" (Hebrews 4:15)

"You know that He appeared in order to take away sins, <u>and in Him there is no sin.</u>" (1 John 3:5)

"No temptation has overtaken you that is not common to man. God is faithful, and He will not let you be tempted beyond your ability, but with the temptation He will also provide the way of escape, that you may be able to endure it." (1 Corinthians 10:13)

The temptations we endure are not unique; they are common. Yet when a man is tempted with pornography, he often says things like, "Why doesn't God deliver me from this? Why doesn't He help me more? I cannot resist these temptations!" But these are the words of a man sinking into self-pity. He is forgetting that these temptations are "common." But he is also neglecting the fact that God is "faithful." God is trustworthy. You can count on Him. He will never be too busy for you. He will never leave you to fend for yourself. He will not only "provide" the way of escape (from your sin, not just from the trial), but He will give you sufficient grace to "endure" this trial as long as necessary.

It would be a mistake to think that we "cannot help ourselves" in the midst of temptation. Don't see yourself as a powerless victim:

"Beloved, I urge you as sojourners and exiles to <u>abstain</u> from the passions of the flesh, which wage war against your soul." (1 Peter 2:11)

"But I say, walk by the Spirit, and you <u>will not</u> gratify the desires of the flesh." (Galatians 5:16)

We are called to fight against the lusts of the flesh and against the temptations of the devil. We can indeed "abstain" from them through the super-abounding grace of God working in us (Remember Romans 5:20-21 that we discussed in Chapter 4). When we walk by the power that resides within us from the Spirit of the Living God, the promise is that we "will not" give in to the desires of the flesh.

"Commit your work to the Lord, and your plans (thoughts) will be established." (Proverbs 16:3)

Here we are reminded of the "conditional" protection that God offers to us. Independence from God will lead to the destruction of our contentment and peace.[62] Too often we fret about being alone, being bored, being filled with lust – yet we do not actively and intentionally "commit our work to the Lord." We do more grumbling and complaining about our state, than crying out to God about our estate. Until we commit our ways to Him, we will not get peace.

---

[62] Bridges, *Proverbs*, 198.

If we try to fight off the temptations of the devil on our own, we will lose the battle for sure. Make your fears known to God through prayer and He will deliver you. Make the Holy Spirit "the censor of your thoughts" and you will not fall into various sins.[63]

Therefore, when we do in fact give in to sin, we know for certain that we are not walking by the power of the Holy Spirit (Chapter 3). God has not let you down or failed to supply sufficient grace.

"*See to it that no one fails to obtain the grace of God...*" (Hebrews 12:15, ESV)

"*See to it that there is no one among you who forfeits the grace of God...*" (Hebrews 12:15, NEB)

We note here that it is indeed possible to "fall short" or to "forfeit" the grace that God supplies. It is not that God didn't do enough to help you in the midst of your temptations. Rather, you made a decision that you would not utilize the grace that God has supplied to you – just like He has for every other believer. You "forfeited" this grace and decided not to allow the power of God to work in you. You have chosen sin instead of grace.

As we discussed in Chapter 1, the devil's work is "condemnation" and the Holy Spirit's work is "conviction." We could also say that the Holy Spirit is first a sanctifier and then a comforter, while the devil is first a tempter and then a troubler.[64] The devil works much like Potipher's wife did with Joseph.

---

[63] William Gurnall, *The Christian in Complete Armour*, Vol. 1, (originally published in 1655; reprint Carlisle, PA: Banner of Truth Trust, 1994), 199.

[64] Gurnall, 96.

First, she tried to lure Joseph into sin to satisfy her own lusts, and then when he rejected her temptations she became the accuser and even used his own cloak to condemn him (see Genesis 39). This is how the enemy of our souls often operates – first as a tempter and then as an accuser. The devil wears multiple "hats" in how he works his temptations.[65] One "hat" he wears is that of the "tempter" and another one he wears is that of the "accuser." He will lure a man into pornographic sin, and then once he falls into it, the enemy will accuse him and condemn him of his wickedness. "Until we have sinned, Satan is a parasite; when we have sinned he is a tyrant."[66] Don't mistakenly think that just attending church services and listening to good sermons will rescue you. Remember that the devil is at church just as often as you are.

We have seen earlier in this chapter how Scripture describes him as a "tempter," let's also note how Scripture describes him as an "accuser."

The Devil is an "Accuser"

"...the accuser of our brothers has been thrown down, who accuses them day and night before our God." (Revelation 12:10)

"Then the Lord showed me Joshua the high priest standing before the angel of the Lord, and Satan standing at his right hand to accuse him." (Zechariah 3:1)

---

[65] Gurnall, vol 1, 82f.

[66] Brooks, 17.

"Simon, Simon, behold, Satan demanded to have you (plural – all of the disciples), that he might sift you (plural – all of the disciples) like wheat, but I have prayed for you (singular – Peter) that your (singular – Peter) faith may not fail. And when you (singular – Peter) have turned again, strengthen your (singular – Peter) brothers." (Luke 22:31-32)

"...fall into the condemnation of the devil..." (1 Timothy 3:6)

The devil works in such a way that he will lure and tempt someone into viewing pornography. And then once that man has fallen into sin, the "tempter" becomes the "accuser" – he switches hats. Now he pummels the sinful soul with guilt, with condemnation, with a "how could you do that" impression upon the soul. And sometimes even with the thought that "you aren't even a believer if you would do that."

We must not neglect spiritual warfare. This is especially true in your battle against pornography. If you don't practice what you have seen in this Chapter, you are too dismissive of the devil as C.S. Lewis warned.

Some Final Thoughts

The title of this book may seem contradictory – porn "murders" yet your soul commits "suicide." So, which is it – murder or suicide? Actually it is both. There is no contradiction here – the enemy of our souls uses pornography to "murder" us, yet it is we ourselves who hang ourselves with it.

Pornography is a murderer, but it doesn't just murder in isolation. It murders romance. It murders a relationship with your spouse. It murders your ability to parent your children with integrity. It murders holiness. It murders a relationship with God. It murders contentment. It murders peace. It murders your own soul.

But pornography is also suicide to the soul. It is self-destructive. You yourself hollow out your own soul. You snuff out the life of the Holy Spirit in your own soul. You kill a relationship with your spouse – and with your God.

And the devil "helps" with both murder and suicide as we saw in the last chapter. But we must not blame the devil (or a cold spouse) for this sin. Even if the devil didn't exist, this sin would trouble mankind. Even if you had a different spouse, you would still have this same problem. It's in your own heart – it's not "out there."

But condemning yourself about this will not prove to be helpful. There is only one response that will help you. Repentance. Turn away from this sin. Leave this sin behind and do not turn back to it again. Do it today. Delay no longer. Don't put your head in the sand ("it's not that bad"). Don't put your head in the noose. As I keyboard these words, I am crying out to God on your behalf and asking for the power of the Holy Spirit to flood your soul and convince and convict you. I have seen God deliver men and women from every type of sin – some that are so depraved that I don't even want to type them out. There is hope for you. And your only hope is from Jesus Christ and the good news of the gospel that He offers you. It won't help you apart from the power of the Holy Spirit. Freedom won't come to you any other way.

"Your iniquities have made a separation between you and your God." (Isaiah 59:2)

Your fellowship with God is destroyed by this sin. You may be a very religious person. You may be doing many good deeds. You may mistakenly believe that "doing good" balances the scales of "doing wrong." But it does not. You are saved by grace, not by your works. You are saved by Jesus Christ and HIS sacrifice on the cross, not by your good intentions. But in saying this about grace, it does not imply that you can continue living the way you are currently living. Only through a deep, humble, abiding walk with God will you know the joys of freedom. This is not an appeal to "get stronger," rather it is an appeal to "get weaker."

"(Jesus said) My grace is sufficient for you, for My power is made perfect in weakness. (Paul responded) Therefore I will boast all the more gladly of my weaknesses, <u>so that</u> the power of Christ may rest upon me." (2 Corinthians 12:9)

Trying harder won't bring you to freedom any more than it would have brought Paul freedom from his thorn in the flesh (12:7). You are gripped by pride. You need to be gripped by your weakness – your own helplessness and inability to overcome this sin (or any other) by your own strength. So rather than telling you to "toughen up," I instead urge you to "weaken up." This is what makes the good news so good. The good news is not for good guys; it's for broken ones.

Learn to be thankful. Express gratitude to the God Who created you. There is an intimate connection between "lust" and "ingratitude." They go hand in hand.

"But sexual immorality and all impurity or covetousness must not even be named among you, as is proper among saints. Let there be no filthiness nor foolish talk nor crude joking, which are out of place, but instead let there be thanksgiving. (Ephesians 5:3-4)

Likewise, those engaged in sexual perversion (Romans 1:24-27) are also described as those who *"although they knew God, they did not honor Him as God or give thanks."* (Romans 1:21)

Finally, I would urge you to pick up my other book that is being published at the same time as this one. It is entitled, *The Beauty of Biblical Meditation – Counseling Your Mind Through the Scriptures*[67]. The reason I suggest this is not because of increased royalties for myself (my books are unlikely to ever be best sellers), but rather because in my decades involved in biblical counseling, I have never seen people change as rapidly or as readily as those who learn how to truly "meditate" (not just memorize) on the Scriptures. I wrote this book on pornography and that book on meditation nearly simultaneously because they are so intimately intertwined. Obviously though, not all who need to learn to meditate struggle with pornography so this is the reason for two books rather than one.

In closing, *"I commend you to God and to the word of His grace, which is able to build you up and to give you the inheritance among all those who are sanctified."* (Acts 20:32)

Soli Deo Gloria

---

[67] For a fuller treatment of this see my book, "The Beauty of Biblical Meditation," available now on www.Amazon.com.